A CourseGuide for

Greek Grammar Beyond the Basics

Daniel B. Wallace

ZONDERVAN ACADEMIC

ZONDERVAN ACADEMIC

A CourseGuide for Greek Grammar Beyond the Basics

Copyright © 2019 by Daniel B. Wallace

ISBN 978-0-310-11062-0 (softcover)

Requests for information should be addressed to:
Zondervan, 3900 Sparks Dr. SE, Grand Rapids, Michigan 49546

All Scripture quotations, unless otherwise indicated, are taken from The Holy Bible, New International Version®, NIV®. Copyright © 1973, 1978, 1984, 2011 by Biblica, Inc.® Used by permission of Zondervan. All rights reserved worldwide. www.Zondervan.com. The "NIV" and "New International Version" are trademarks registered in the United States Patent and Trademark Office by Biblica, Inc.®

Any internet addresses (websites, blogs, etc.) and telephone numbers in this book are offered as a resource. They are not intended in any way to be or imply an endorsement by Zondervan, nor does Zondervan vouch for the content of these sites and numbers for the life of this book.

No part of this publication may be reproduced, stored in a retrieval system, or transmitted in any form or by any means—electronic, mechanical, photocopy, recording, or any other—except for brief quotations in printed reviews, without the prior permission of the publisher.

Printed in the United States of America

CONTENTS

Introduction 5

1. **Nominative and Vocative** 7
2. **Genitive** 11
3. **Dative** 15
4. **Accusative** 19
5. **Article (Part I, Origin, Function, Regular Uses, Absence of Article)** 23
6. **Article (Part II, Special Uses and Non-Uses of the Article)** 27
7. **Adjectives** 31
8. **Person and Number, Active Voice** 35
9. **Middle and Passive Voice** 39
10. **The Indicative Mood** 43
11. **The Subjunctive Mood** 47
12. **The Optative and Imperative Moods** 51
13. **The Present Tense** 55
14. **The Imperfect Tense** 59
15. **The Aorist and Future Tenses** 63

16. The Perfect and Pluperfect Tenses 67

17. The Infinitive 71

18. The Participle (Part I) 75

19. The Participle (Part II) 79

20. Conditional Sentences 84

Introduction

Welcome to the A CourseGuide for Greek Grammar Beyond the Basics. These guides were created for formal and informal students alike who want to engage deeper in biblical, theological, or ministry studies. We hope this guide will provide an opportunity for you to grow not only in your understanding, but also in your faith.

How to Use this Guide

This guide is meant to be used in conjunction with the book *Greek Grammar Beyond the Basics* and its corresponding videos, *Greek Grammar Beyond the Basics Video Lectures*. After you have read each chapter in the book and watched the accompanying video lesson, the materials in this guide will help you review and assess what you have learned. Application-oriented questions are included as well. For additional practice, you will want to complete exercises found in *A Workbook for New Testament Syntax*.

Each CourseGuide has been individually designed to best equip you in your studies, but in general, you can expect the following components. Most CourseGuides begin every chapter with a "You Should Know" section, which highlights key terminology, people, and facts to remember. This section serves as a helpful summary for directing your studies. Reflection questions, typically two to three per chapter, prompt you to summarize key points you've learned. Discussion questions invite you to an even deeper level of engagement. Finally, most chapters will end with a short quiz to test your retention. You can find the answer key to each quiz at the bottom of the page following it.

For Further Study

CourseGuides accompany books and videos from some of the world's top biblical and theological scholars. They may be used independently, or in small groups or classrooms, offering quality instruction to equip students for academic and ministry pursuits. If you would like to engage in further study with Zondervan's Course-Guides, the full lineup may be viewed online. After completing your studies with *A CourseGuide for Greek Grammar Beyond the Basics,* we recommend moving on to *A CourseGuide for Basics of Biblical Hebrew* and *A CourseGuide for Basics of Biblical Aramaic.*

CHAPTER 1

Nominative and Vocative

You Should Know

- The substantive in the nominative case is frequently the subject of a finite verb. The verb may be explicitly stated or implied.

- The predicate nominative (PN) is approximately the same as the subject (S) and is joined to it by an equative verb, whether stated or implied.

- The predicate nominative (PN) is approximately the same as the subject (S) and is joined to it by an equative verb, whether stated or implied.

- The nominative case can be an appositive to another substantive in the same case.

- The nominative case can be an appositive to another substantive in the same case.

- The nominative absolute is the use of the nominative case in introductory material, which are not to be construed as sentences.

- A parenthetic nominative is actually the subject in a clause inside a sentence that may or may not have a different subject.

- A substantive in the nominative is used in the place of the vocative case. It is used (as is the voc.) in direct address to designate the addressee.

- A substantive in the vocative is used in direct address to designate the addressee.

- What is the best translation for the word παραγίνομαι?
  - I appear, come, arrive
- What is the best translation for the word ἔρημος?
  - Wilderness
- What is the best translation for the word μαρτυρία?
  - Testimony, witness
- What is the best translation for the word καταγγέλλω?
  - I proclaim, announce
- What is the best translation for the word εὐχαριστέω?
  - I give thanks
- What is the best translation for the word θυγάτηρ?
  - Daughter
- What is the best translation for the word πολλάκις?
  - Often, many times
- What is the best translation for the word κλητός?
  - Elect
- What is the best translation for the word διάκονος?
  - Servant, minister
- What is the best translation for the word ἄχρι?
  - Until

Quiz

1. The best definition of the subjective nominative is:
    a) The subject of a finite verb
    b) The object of a finite verb
    c) A verbal noun
    d) The noun that receives the action of the main verb

2. The best description of the vocative case is:
   a) It is used to express an indirect object of a verb
   b) It is used in direct address
   c) It is only used in relative clauses
   d) It is used only as the subject of an imperative verb

3. What is the best description of the nominatives in this phrase from the title of the letter to the Philippians: **Τιμόθεος δοῦλοι** Χριστοῦ Ἰησοῦ?
   a) Nominative for vocative
   b) Parenthetic nominative
   c) Nominative absolute
   d) Nominative in simple apposition

4. What is the best description of the nominative ὄνομα in this phrase: Ἐγένετο ἄνθρωπος, ἀπεσταλμένος παρὰ θεοῦ, **ὄνομα** αὐτῷ Ἰωάννης?
   a) Subject nominative
   b) Predicate nominative
   c) Parenthetic nominative
   d) Nominative in simple apposition

5. What is the best description of the nominative ὁ υἱός in this phrase: οὗτός ἐστιν **ὁ υἱὸς** τοῦ θεοῦ?
   a) Subject nominative for vocative
   b) Parenthetic nominative
   c) Nominative in simple apposition
   d) Predicate nominative

6. What is the best description of the nominative in this phrase: ἠγέρθη **Χριστὸς** ἐκ νεκρῶν?
   a) Nominative for vocative
   b) Parenthetic nominative
   c) Subject nominative
   d) Nominative in simple apposition

7. What is the best description of the nominatives in this phrase from the title of Romans: **Παῦλος δοῦλος** Χριστοῦ Ἰησοῦ?

a) Nominative absolute
b) Nominative for vocative
c) Parenthetic nominative
d) Nominative in simple apposition

8. What is the best description of the nominative in this phrase: οἶδά σου τὴν θλῖψιν καὶ τὴν πτωχείαν, ἀλλὰ **πλούσιος** εἶ?
    a) Subject nominative
    b) Parenthetic nominative
    c) Predicate nominative
    d) Nominative in simple apposition

9. What is the best description of the **first** nominative in this phrase: **πνεῦμα** ὁ θεός?
    a) Subject nominative for vocative
    b) *Nominativus pendens* (pendent nominative)
    c) Nominative in simple apposition
    d) Predicate nominative

10. What is the best description of the nominative in this phrase: **Ὁ νικῶν** ποιήσω αὐτὸν στῦλον?
    a) *Nominativus pendens* (pendent nominative)
    b) Parenthetic nominative
    c) Nominative in simple apposition
    d) Predicate nominative

Answer Key

1. A, 2. B, 3. C, 4. C, 5. D, 6. C, 7. A, 8. B, 9. D, 10. A

CHAPTER 2

Genitive

You Should Know

- Descriptive genitive: The genitive substantive describes the head noun in a loose manner. It's the "catch-all" genitive. For the word *of* insert the paraphrase "characterized by" or "described by."

- Possessive genitive: The substantive in the genitive possesses the thing to which it stands related.

- Partitive genitive: The substantive in the genitive denotes the whole of which the head noun is a part. For the word "of" you can substitute "which is a part of."

- Attributive genitive: The genitive substantive specifies an attribute or innate quality of the head substantive. If the noun in the genitive can be converted into an attributive adjective, then the genitive is likely an attributive genitive.

- The genitive substantive specifies an attribute or innate quality of the head substantive.

- Simple apposition requires that both nouns be in the same case.

- Apposition genitive: The substantive in the genitive case refers to the same thing as the substantive to which it is related. Replace the word "of" with the paraphrase "which is" or "that is, namely."

- Comparison genitive: The genitive substantive, almost always after a comparative adjective, is used to indicate comparison. This requires the word "than" before the genitive (instead of the usual "of").

- Subjective genitive: The genitive substantive functions semantically as the subject of the verbal idea implicit in the head noun.

- Objective genitive: The genitive substantive functions semantically as the direct object of the verbal idea implicit in the head noun.

- What is the best translation for the word ἅπτω?
  - I touch, take hold of

- What is the best translation for the word διακονέω?
  - I serve, minister to

- What is the best translation for the word κρίσις?
  - Judgment

- What is the best translation for the word φυλή?
  - Tribe

- What is the best translation for the word δέησις?
  - Prayer

- What is the best translation for the word σωτηρία?
  - Salvation, deliverance

- What is the best translation for the word κλῆσις?
  - Call, calling

- What is the best translation for the word ἐπίγνωσις?
  - Knowledge

- What is the best translation for the word προσευχή?
  - Prayer

- What is the best translation for the word αὐξάνω?
  - I cause to grow, increase

Quiz

1. Which of the following best describes the genitive in this phrase: αὐτοῦ τὸ ὠτίον? (ὠτίον, ear)?

a) Genitive of relationship
   b) Possessive genitive
   c) Attributive genitive
   d) Genitive of simple apposition

2. The attributive genitive:
   a) Describes the head word as part of a whole
   b) Is only used after an attributive adjective
   c) Specifies an innate quality of the head substantive
   d) Describes the kind of time within which an action takes place

3. The subjective genitive:
   a) Functions semantically as the subject of a verbal idea implicit in the head noun
   b) Defines the source of the head noun
   c) Functions semantically to mark the kind of time within which an action takes place
   d) Describes an association between the genitive and the head noun

4. The objective genitive:
   a) Describes the genitive as subordinate to the head noun
   b) Functions semantically as the object of a verbal idea implicit in the head noun
   c) Specifies an innate quality of the head substantive
   d) Functions semantically as the direct object of certain verbs

5. Which of the following best describes the genitive in this phrase: οὕτως ἔσται ἡ παρουσία **τοῦ υἱοῦ** τοῦ ἀνθρώπου?
   a) Objective genitive
   b) Subjective genitive
   c) Attributive genitive
   d) Genitive of relationship

6. Which of the following best describes the genitive in this phrase: ἡ δὲ **τοῦ πνεύματος** βλασφημία οὐκ ἀφεθήσεται? (οὐκ ἀφεθήσεται = "will not be forgiven")

a) Genitive of relationship
   b) Attributive genitive
   c) Objective genitive
   d) Subjective genitive

7. Which of the following best describes the genitive in this phrase: τῷ λαῷ **τοῦ θεοῦ**?
   a) Genitive of relationship
   b) Attributive genitive
   c) Possessive genitive
   d) Genitive of simple apposition

8. Which of the following best describes the genitive in this phrase: τὸ δέκατον (one tenth) **τῆς πόλεως**?
   a) Genitive of relationship
   b) Partitive genitive
   c) Attributive genitive
   d) Genitive of simple apposition

9. Which of the following best describes the genitive in this phrase: τὸ μωρὸν τοῦ θεοῦ σοφώτερον **τῶν ἀνθρώπων** ἐστίν?
   a) Genitive of relationship
   b) Genitive of comparison
   c) Attributive genitive
   d) Genitive of simple apposition

10. Which of the following best describes the genitive in this phrase: παρέλαβεν τὸ παιδίον καὶ τὴν μητέρα αὐτοῦ **νυκτός**?
    a) Genitive of relationship
    b) Genitive of time
    c) Attributive genitive
    d) Genitive of simple apposition

ANSWER KEY

1. B, 2. C, 3. A, 4. B, 5. B, 6. C, 7. C, 8. B, 9. B, 10. B

CHAPTER 3

Dative

You Should Know

- Dative of indirect object: The dative substantive is that to or for which the action of a verb is performed.

- Dative of interest: The dative substantive indicates the person (or, rarely, thing) interested in the verbal action.

- Dative of reference: The dative substantive is that in reference to which something is presented as true. Supply the phrase "with reference to" before the dative.

- Dative of simple apposition: The dative case can be an appositive to another substantive in the same case.

- Dative of sphere: The dative substantive indicates the sphere or realm in which the word to which it is related takes place or exists. Before the noun in the dative, supply the words *in the sphere of* or *in the realm of*.

- Dative of time: The noun in the dative indicates the time when the action of the main verb is accomplished. The dative of time expresses a point in time.

- Dative of manner: The dative substantive denotes the manner in which the action of the verb is accomplished. Supply *with* or *in* before the dative noun.

- Dative of means: The dative substantive is used to indicate the means or instrument by which the verbal action is accomplished. Before the noun in the dative, supply the words *by means of*, or simply *with*.

- Dative of agency: The dative substantive is used to indicate the personal agent by whom the action of the verb is accomplished.

- Dative of content: The noun in the dative denotes the content that is used by a verb of filling.

- What is the best translation for the word ἑτοιμάζω?
  - I prepare

- What is the best translation for the word καινός?
  - New

- What is the best translation for the word διώκω?
  - I persecute, pursue

- What is the best translation for the word συνέρχομαι?
  - I assemble, gather

- What is the best translation for the word θύρα?
  - Door

- What is the best translation for the word παρρησία?
  - Confidence, boldness

- What is the best translation for the word θερίζω?
  - I reap, harvest

- What is the best translation for the word καυχάομαι?
  - I boast, brag

- What is the best translation for the word περιτομή?
  - Circumcision

- What is the best translation for the word βαστάζω?
  - I bear, carry

Quiz

1. The best definition of the dative of reference is:
    a) The dative substantive is used in reference to something which is presented as true

b) The dative substantive is a part of the larger whole indicated by the head noun
c) The dative refers to a specific location in which the noun is placed
d) The dative refers to possession of qualities of the head noun

2. What is the best description of the relationship of the datives in this phrase: Δρουσίλλῃ τῇ ἰδίᾳ γυναικὶ?
   a) Dative on relationship
   b) Dative in simple apposition
   c) Dative of means
   d) Dative of reference

3. What is the best description of the datives in this phrase: **τῇ τρίτῃ ἡμέρᾳ** ἐγερθήσεται (he will rise)?
   a) Dative of time
   b) Dative of means
   c) Dative of relationship
   d) Dative of reference

4. What is the best description of the dative in this phrase: ἐκμάξασα (she wiped) τοὺς πόδας αὐτοῦ **ταῖς θριξὶν** αὐτῆς?
   a) Dative of location
   b) Dative of means
   c) Dative of agency
   d) Dative of manner

5. What is the best description of the dative in this phrase: μόνον ἵνα **τῷ σταυρῷ** τοῦ Χριστοῦ μὴ διώκωνται?
   a) Dative of reference
   b) Dative of time
   c) Dative of cause
   d) Dative of indirect object

6. What is the best description of the bolded dative in this phrase: ἐδόθη **μοι** σκόλοψ τῇ σαρκί?
   a) Dative of interest
   b) Dative of time

c) Dative in simple apposition
d) Dative of indirect object

7. What is the best description of the dative in this phrase: μακάριοι οἱ καθαροὶ **τῇ καρδίᾳ**?

    a) Dative of interest
    b) Dative of time
    c) Dative in simple apposition
    d) Dative of reference

8. What is the best description of the dative in this phrase: οἱ πτωχοὶ **τῷ πνεύματι**?

    a) Dative of place
    b) Dative of sphere
    c) Dative in simple apposition
    d) Dative of reference

9. What is the best description of the dative in this phrase: συνεζωοποίησεν **τῷ Χριστῷ**?

    a) Dative of association
    b) Dative of time
    c) Dative in direct object
    d) Dative of content

10. What is the best description of the second dative in this phrase: ταῦτά σοι πάντα δώσω, ἐὰν πεσὼν προσκυνήσῃς **μοι**?

    a) Dative of interest
    b) Dative of time
    c) Dative in simple apposition
    d) Dative of direct object

ANSWER KEY

1. A, 2. B, 3. A, 4. B, 5. C, 6. D, 7. D, 8. B, 9. A, 10. D

CHAPTER 4

Accusative

You Should Know

- Accusative of direct object: The accusative substantive indicates the immediate object of the action of a transitive verb.

- Double accusative of the person and thing: Certain verbs take two direct objects, one a person and the other a thing.

- Double accusative of object-complement: One accusative substantive is the direct object of the verb and the other accusative complements the object in that it predicates something about it.

- Accusative subject of infinitive: The accusative substantive frequently functions semantically as the subject of the infinitive.

- Accusative in simple apposition: The accusative case can be an appositive to another substantive in the same case.

- Accusative of measure: The accusative substantive indicates the extent of the verbal action. Supply before the accusative *for the extent of* or (with reference to time) *for the duration of*.

- What is the best translation for the word κύων?
  - Dog

- What is the best translation for the word λατρεύω?
  - I serve, worship

- What is the best translation for the word κερδαίνω?
  - I gain, profit

- What is the best translation for the word ἀνάστασις?
  - Resurrection

- What is the best translation for the word ζῆλος?
  - Zeal, ardor, jealousy
- What is the best translation for the word περισσεύω?
  - I abound, surpass, overflow
- What is the best translation for the word δοκιμάζω?
  - I put to the test
- What is the best translation for the word ἔπαινος?
  - Praise, approval, recognition
- What is the best translation for the word δεσμός?
  - Prisoner
- What is the best translation for the word φανερός?
  - Visible, clear

Quiz

1. The best definition of the accusative case is:
    a) The case of qualification (or limitation) and (occasionally) separation
    b) The case of personal interest, reverence, position, and means
    c) The case of extent, direction, or goal
    d) The case of direct address

2. What is the best description of the second accusative in this phrase: πίστευσον ἐπὶ τὸν κύριον Ἰησοῦν?
    a) Accusative of direct object
    b) Accusative in simple apposition
    c) Accusative of means
    d) Accusative of reference

3. What is the best description of the accusative in this phrase: νηστεύσας **ἡμέρας** τεσσεράκοντα?
    a) Accusative of measure (extent of time)
    b) Accusative of means

c) Accusative of direct object
d) Adverbial accusative

4. What is the best description of the accusatives in this phrase: ἐκεῖνος ὑμᾶς διδάξει (will teach) πάντα?

   a) Accusative of means
   b) Accusative of measure (extent of space)
   c) Double accusative
   d) Predicate accusative

5. Which of the following is an example of accusative as an object-complement?

   a) ἐποίησεν τὸ ὕδωρ οἶνον
   b) οὐκ ἦλθον καλέσαι δικαίους
   c) δωρεὰν ἐλάβετε
   d) Μωϋσῆς γὰρ γράφει τὴν δικαιοσύνη

6. What is the best description of the accusative in this phrase: τοῦ γνῶναι **αὐτὸν**?

   a) Accusative reference
   b) Double accusative
   c) Accusative of direct object
   d) Predicate accusative

7. What is the best description of the accusative in this phrase: Ἀνδρέαν **τὸν ἀδελφὸν** Σίμωνος?

   a) Accusative of direct object
   b) Accusative of means
   c) Accusative in simple apposition
   d) Accusative of reference

8. What is the best description of the accusative in this phrase: ἦλθον ἡμέρας **ὁδὸν**?

   a) Accusative subject of infinitive
   b) Accusative of measure (extent of space)
   c) Accusative of means
   d) Adverbial accusative

9. What is the best description of the accusative in this phrase: ἄφετε **τὰ παιδία** ἔρχεσθαι πρός με?

   a) Accusative object of infinitive
   b) Accusative of measure (extent of space)
   c) Accusative subject of infinitive
   d) Predicate accusative

10. What is the best description of the accusatives in this phrase: οὐκ ἦλθον καλέσαι **δικαίους** ἀλλὰ **ἁμαρτωλούς**?

    a) Accusative of means
    b) Accusative of measure (extent of space)
    c) Accusative direct object
    d) Predicate accusative

ANSWER KEY
1. C, 2. B, 3. A, 4. C, 5. A, 6. C, 7. C, 8. B, 9. C, 10. C

CHAPTER 5

Article (Part I, Origin, Function, Regular Uses, Absence of Article)

You Should Know

- The article intrinsically has the ability to *conceptualize*. It is used predominantly to stress the *identity* of an individual or class or quality. It also serves a determining function at times—it *definitizes*.

- As a relative pronoun: Sometimes the article is equivalent to a relative pronoun in force. To say that the article is functioning like a relative pronoun is only an English way of looking at the matter.

- Anaphoric: The anaphoric article is the article denoting previous reference.

- Deictic ("pointing" article): The article is occasionally used to point out an object or person which/who is present at the moment of speaking.

- *Par excellence*: The article is frequently used to point out a substantive that is, in a sense, "in a class by itself." But it is not necessarily used just for the *best* of a class. It could be used for the *worst* of a class.

- Monadic ("one of a kind" or "unique" article): The article is frequently used to identify monadic or one-of-a-kind nouns, such as "the devil," "the sun," "the Christ."

- Well-known ("celebrity"): The article points out an object that is well-known, but for reasons other than the above categories.

- Abstract: Abstract nouns by their very nature focus on a quality. However, when such a noun is articular, that quality is defined more closely. In translating such nouns, the article should rarely be used.

- With Adjectives: Adjectives often stand in the place of nouns, especially when the qualities of a particular group are stressed.

- It is not necessary for a noun to have the article in order for it to be definite. When a substantive is *anarthrous* (no article), it may have one of three forces: indefinite, qualitative, or definite.

- What is the best translation for the word δυνατός?
  - Powerful, strong, mighty, able

- What is the best translation for the word δέσμιος?
  - Prisoner

- What is the best translation for the word πλοῦτος?
  - Riches, wealth, abundance

- What is the best translation for the word μυστήριον?
  - Secret, mystery

- What is the best translation for the word νοέω?
  - I perceive, apprehend, understand

- What is the best translation for the word κτίζω?
  - I create

- What is the best translation for the word οὐκέτι?
  - No longer, no more

- What is the best translation for the word σωτήρ?
  - Savior, deliverer

- What is the best translation for the word ἀληθῶς?
  - Truly, in truth

- What is the best translation for the word οἰκοδομή?
  - Building (up), construction

Quiz

1. The article in Greek *intrinsically* has the ability to:
   a) Conceptualize
   b) Itemize nouns
   c) Provide structure and order
   d) Create qualitative differences between nouns

2. The article in this phrase functions as what kind of pronoun? Πάτερ ἡμῶν **ὁ** ἐν τοῖς οὐρανοῖς
   a) Personal pronoun
   b) Relative pronoun
   c) Possessive pronoun
   d) Demonstrative pronoun

3. The article in this phrase functions as what kind of pronoun? **Οἱ** δὲ εἶπαν πρὸς αὐτόν
   a) Relative pronoun
   b) Possessive pronoun
   c) Personal pronoun
   d) Demonstrative pronoun

4. What is the best description of the article in this phrase: μακάριοι **οἱ** *πραεῖς* (meek)?
   a) As a substantiver, the adjective functions as a noun
   b) It distinguishes the subject from the predicate nominative
   c) It highlights some quality of the noun
   d) The noun is "well known" (the "celebrity" article)

5. What does the *absence of an article* on the word ἀγάπη indicate for this phrase: ὁ θεὸς ***ἀγάπη*** ἐστίν?
   a) That the adjective is the indirect object
   b) That the adjective is a quality or trait of the noun
   c) That the adjective is an activity or action of the noun
   d) That the adjective should be understood as a proper noun

6. The article in this phrase functions as what kind of pronoun? καὶ τὴν δόξαν **τὴν** παρὰ τοῦ μόνου θεοῦ οὐ ζητεῖτε;

a) Personal pronoun
b) Relative pronoun
c) Possessive pronoun
d) Demonstrative pronoun

7. What is the best description of the article in this phrase: ὁ προφήτης εἶ σύ;?

a) *Par excellence*
b) Monadic
c) Well-known, celebrity
d) Abstract

8. What is the best description of the article in this phrase: πειρασθῆναι ὑπὸ **τοῦ** διαβόλου?

a) *Par excellence*
b) Monadic
c) Relative pronoun
d) Abstract

9. What is the best description of the article in this phrase: Ὁ πρεσβύτερος ἐκλεκτῇ κυρίᾳ καὶ τοῖς τέκνοις αὐτῆς?

a) *Par excellence*
b) Person pronoun
c) Well-known, celebrity
d) Abstract

10. What is the best description of the article in this phrase: ὅτι ἡ σωτηρία ἐκ τῶν Ἰουδαίων ἐστίν?

a) *Par excellence*
b) Monadic
c) Well-known, celebrity
d) Abstract

ANSWER KEY

1. A, 2. B, 3. C, 4. A, 5. B, 6. B, 7. A, 8. B, 9. C, 10. D

Article (Part II, Special Uses and Non-Uses of the Article)

You Should Know

- Colwell's rule: An anarthrous pre-verbal predicate nominative is a predicate nominative that does not have the article and occurs before the equative verb. An anarthrous pre-verbal PN is normally qualitative, sometimes definite, and only rarely indefinite.

- Granville Sharp rule (TSKS): When two nouns are connected by καί and the article precedes only the first noun, there is a close connection between the two. TSKS—article, substantive, καί, substantive

- *When the construction meets three specific demands*, then the two nouns always refer to the same person: neither is impersonal; neither is plural; neither is a proper name.

- Anarthrous: without the article

- Pre-verbal: before the equative verb (εἰμί, γίνομαι)

- Predicate nominative (PN): the noun in the nominative case that is the same as the subject (more or less)

- What is the best translation for the word ἐκεῖθεν?
  - From there

- What is the best translation for the word τιμή?
  - Value, honor

- What is the best translation for the word ἑορτή?
  - Festival
- What is the best translation for the word ἀσθενέω?
  - I am weak, sick, powerless
- What is the best translation for the word οἶνος?
  - Wine
- What is the best translation for the word ἰάομαι?
  - I heal, cure, restore
- What is the best translation for the word μήν?
  - Month, new moon
- What is the best translation for the word τίκτω?
  - I give birth to, bear
- What is the best translation for the word παρθένος?
  - Virgin

Quiz

1. When a word is used without an article, it is called:
   a) Contextual
   b) Epexegetical
   c) Anarthrous
   d) Substantival

2. Colwell's rule is:
   a) Definite predicate nouns which follow the verb usually lack the article
   b) Definite predicate nouns which precede the verb usually lack the article
   c) Definite predicate nouns which precede the verb usually have the article
   d) Definite predicate nouns are always anarthrous

3. Granville Sharp's rule states that when the construction is article-substantive-καί-substantive, and neither is impersonal, plural, or proper names, then:
   a) The second substantive refers to the same person mentioned by first substantive
   b) The second substantive refers to a different person mentioned by first substantive
   c) The second substantive gives a formal title to the first substantive
   d) The second substantive describes adjectively first substantive

4. The following phrase is an example of which syntactical rule: ὁ λόγος σὰρξ ἐγένετο?
   a) Colwell's Rule
   b) J. H. Moulton's Rule
   c) Granville Sharp Rule
   d) Apollonius' Corollary

5. The following phrase is an example of which syntactical rule: τὸν ἀπόστολον καὶ ἀρχιερέα τῆς ὁμολογίας ἡμῶν Ἰησοῦν?
   a) Colwell's Rule
   b) Apollonius' Corollary
   c) Granville Sharp Rule
   d) A. T. Robertson's Rule

6. The nouns in this phrase, πνεῦμα θεοῦ, can be described as:
   a) Anarthrous
   b) Contextual
   c) Epexegetical
   d) Substantival

7. The following phrase is an example of which syntactical rule: ὁ θεὸς ἀγάπη ἐστίν?
   a) Colwell's Rule
   b) J. H. Moulton's Rule
   c) Granville Sharp Rule
   d) Apollonius' Corollary

8. The following phrase is an example of which syntactical rule: Ἐπαφρόδιτον τὸν ἀδελφὸν καὶ συνεργὸν καὶ συστρατιώτην μου?

   a) Colwell's Rule
   b) Apollonius' Corollary
   c) Granville Sharp Rule
   d) A. T. Robertson's Rule

9. The following phrase is an example of which syntactical rule: Ὁ λόγος γὰρ ὁ τοῦ σταυροῦ τοῖς... δὲ σῳζομένοις ἡμῖν **δύναμις** θεοῦ ἐστιν?

   a) Granville Sharp Rule
   b) A. T. Robertson's Rule
   c) Colwell's Rule
   d) Apollonius' Corollary

10. The following phrase is an example of which syntactical rule: τοῦ θεοῦ ἡμῶν καὶ σωτῆρος Ἰησοῦ Χριστοῦ?

    a) Colwell's Rule
    b) Apollonius' Corollary
    c) Granville Sharp Rule
    d) A. T. Robertson's Rule

ANSWER KEY

1. C, 2. B, 3. A, 4. A, 5. C, 6. A, 7. A, 8. C, 9. C, 10. C

CHAPTER 7

Adjectives

You Should Know

- Substantival "non-adjectival" uses of the adjective: The adjective is frequently used.

- Adverbial "non-adjectival" uses of the adjective: The adjective is sometimes used in the place of an adverb.

- Superlative for comparative: The superlative can have the same sense as the comparative when it compares only two things rather than three or more.

- The attributive positions: Article-adjective-noun; Article-noun-article-adjective

- The predicate positions: Adjective-article-noun; the adjective seems to be slightly more emphatic than the noun

- The anarthrous adjective-noun construction: Use context to determine attributive or predicate positions.

- What is the best translation for the word θλῖψις?
  - Oppression, affliction, trouble

- What is the best translation for the word νομίζω?
  - I think, believe, hold

- What is the best translation for the word περισσεύω?
  - I abound

- What is the best translation for the word ἐλάχιστος?
  - Least, smallest

- What is the best translation for the word θησαυρός?
  - Repository, treasure, chest
- What is the best translation for the word δένδρον?
  - Tree
- What is the best translation for the word μωρός?
  - Foolish
- What is the best translation for the word δεύτερος?
  - Second
- What is the best translation for the word ἀποδίδωμι?
  - I give up, yield
- What is the best translation for the word καταλύω?
  - I detach, destroy, put to an end

Quiz

1. What is the best description of the adjective in this phrase: ῥῦσαι ἡμᾶς ἀπὸ **τοῦ πονηροῦ**?
   a) Adverbial
   b) Adjectival
   c) Substantival
   d) Relative

2. What is the use of the adjective in this phrase: λέγω δὲ ὑμῖν ὅτι τοῦ ἱεροῦ **μεῖζόν** ἐστιν ὧδε?
   a) Superlative for comparative
   b) Superlative
   c) Comparative
   d) Predicate

3. What is the use of the adjective in this phrase: ἄνθρωπος εἶχεν τέκνα δύο. καὶ προσελθὼν **τῷ πρώτῳ** εἶπεν . . . ?

a) Relative
b) Superlative for comparative
c) Comparative
d) Superlative

4. What is the position of the adjective in this phrase: ἐπέπεσεν **τὸ πνεῦμα τὸ ἅγιον** ἐπ' αὐτούς?

   a) Attributive
   b) Predicate
   c) Comparative
   d) Superlative

5. What is the position of the adjective in this phrase: **μακάριοι** οἱ εἰρηνοποιοί?

   a) Attributive
   b) Predicate
   c) Comparative
   d) Superlative

6. What is the best description of the adjective in this phrase: ὅτι πολλοὶ προφῆται καὶ **δίκαιοι**?

   a) Adverbial
   b) Adjectival
   c) Substantival
   d) Relative

7. What is the use of the adjective in this phrase: καὶ τοὺς **πλείονας** τῶν ἀδελφῶν ἐν κυρίῳ πεποιθότας?

   a) Elative
   b) Superlative
   c) Comparative
   d) Predicate

8. What is the use of the adjective in this phrase: Ἐγὼ γάρ εἰμι ὁ **ἐλάχιστος** τῶν ἀποστόλων?

   a) Relative
   b) Superlative for comparative

c) Comparative
d) Superlative

9. What is the position of the adjective in this phrase: ὅτι ἔκρινεν τὴν πόρνην τὴν **μεγάλην**?
   a) Attributive
   b) Predicate
   c) Comparative
   d) Superlative

10. What is the position of the adjective in this phrase: **καλὸν** τὸ ἅλας?
    a) Attributive
    b) Predicate
    c) Comparative
    d) Superlative

ANSWER KEY
1. C, 2. C, 3. B, 4. A, 5. B, 6. C, 7. C, 8. D, 9. A, 10. B

CHAPTER 8

Person and Number, Active Voice

You Should Know

- In general, a verb usually agrees with the subject in both person and number (known as concord).

- In many situations in the NT, especially in the epistles, the use of *we* is not always clear.

- A neuter plural subject normally takes a singular verb. The singular verb regards the plural subject as a collective whole.

- When two subjects, each in the singular, are joined by a conjunction, the verb is usually in the plural.

- Simple active: The subject performs or experiences the action. The verb may be transitive or intransitive.

- Causative active: The subject is not directly involved in the action, but may be said to be the ultimate source or cause of it.

- Stative active: The subject exists in the state indicated by the verb ("I am x").

- Reflexive active: The subject acts upon himself or herself. In such cases naturally the reflexive pronoun is employed as the direct object (e.g., ἑαυτόν).

- What is the best translation for the word λευκός?
  – Bright, shining, white

- What is the best translation for the word ταπεινόω?
  – I lower, humble

- What is the best translation for the word μέχρι?
  - Until, as far as
- What is the best translation for the word χαρίζομαι?
  - I give graciously, grant
- What is the best translation for the word παύω?
  - I stop, hinder, cease
- What is the best translation for the word ἐπίγνωσις?
  - Knowledge, understanding
- What is the best translation for the word πλήρωμα?
  - That which fills up, full measure
- What is the best translation for the word σκότος?
  - Darkness
- What is the best translation for the word ῥύομαι?
  - I save, rescue, deliver
- What is the best translation for the word εἰκών?
  - Likeness, portrait, image

Quiz

1. What is the best explanation of the apparent discord between the subject and verb in this example: ἦλθεν **τὰ πετεινὰ**?
    a) The editorial we
    b) The inclusive we
    c) Neuter plural subjects take singular verbs
    d) Compound subjects take singular verbs

2. What is the best explanation of the singular verb in this example: **ἐκλήθη** δὲ καὶ ὁ Ἰησοῦς καὶ οἱ μαθηταὶ αὐτοῦ εἰς τὸν γάμον?
    a) Compound subjects take singular verbs
    b) The "literary plural"

c) Neuter plural subjects take singular verbs
d) The "indefinite plural"

3. What is the best explanation of the plural verb in this example: **ἐλάβομεν** χάριν καὶ ἀποστολήν?

   a) The editorial we
   b) The "literary plural"
   c) Neuter plural subjects take singular verbs
   d) The "indefinite plural"

4. What is the best explanation of the active voice in this example: ἡ ἀγάπη μακροθυμεῖ?

   a) Reflexive active
   b) Stative active
   c) Simple active
   d) Causative active

5. What is the best explanation of the active voice in this example: ὁ Πιλᾶτος τὸν Ἰησοῦν καὶ **ἐμαστίγωσεν**?

   a) Reflexive active
   b) Stative active
   c) Simple active
   d) Causative active

6. What is the best explanation of the active voice in this example: σῶσον σεαυτόν?

   a) Reflexive active
   b) Stative active
   c) Simple active
   d) Causative active

7. What is the best explanation of the plural verb in this example: **ἠθελήσαμεν** ἐλθεῖν πρὸς ὑμᾶς?

   a) The "indefinite plural"
   b) The editorial we
   c) The "literary plural"
   d) Neuter plural subjects take singular verbs

8. What is the best explanation of the plural verb in this example: πολλὰ γὰρ **πταίομεν** (stumble) ἅπαντες?

   a) The editorial we
   b) The inclusive we
   c) Neuter plural subjects take singular verbs
   d) Compound subjects take singular verb

9. What is the best explanation of the active voice in this example: οὗτός ἐστιν ὁ πλάνος καὶ ὁ ἀντίχριστος?

   a) Reflexive active
   b) Stative active
   c) Simple active
   d) Causative active

ANSWER KEY
1. C, 2. A, 3. A, 4. B, 5. D, 6. A, 7. B, 8. B, 9. B

CHAPTER 9

Middle and Passive Voice

You Should Know

- In general, in the middle voice the subject performs or experiences the action expressed by the verb in such a way that emphasizes the *subject's participation*. It may be said that the subject acts "with a vested interest."

- Not infrequently the difference between the active and middle of the same verb is more lexical than grammatical.

- Direct middle (reflexive or direct reflexive): The subject acts on himself or herself.

- Indirect middle (indirect reflexive): The subject acts for (or sometimes by) himself or herself, or in his or her own interest.

- Deponent middle: A deponent middle is a middle voice verb that has no active form but is active in meaning. The simplest procedure is to consider a middle (or passive) to be deponent if the lexical form of the word in BAGD is middle (or passive), not active.

- In the passive voice the subject is acted upon or receives the action expressed by the verb. No volition—nor even necessarily awareness of the action—is implied on the part of the subject. The subject may or may not be aware; its volition may or may not be involved.

- Simple passive: The subject receives the action.

- Deponent passive: A verb that has no active form may be active in meaning though passive in form.

- What is the best translation for the word ἐπιτιμάω?
  - I rebuke, warn
- What is the best translation for the word διότι?
  - Because, therefore
- What is the best translation for the word γνωρίζω?
  - I know, make known
- What is the best translation for the word κεῖμαι?
  - I lie, recline, be appointed
- What is the best translation for the word πάντοτε?
  - Always, at all times
- What is the best translation for the word οἷος?
  - Of what sort
- What is the best translation for the word δέησις?
  - Prayer
- What is the best translation for the word αἱρέω (in the middle)?
  - I choose, prefer
- What is the best translation for the word καύχημα?
  - Boast, object of boasting
- What is the best translation for the word σωτηρία?
  - Deliverance, salvation

Quiz

1. A verb in the middle voice:
   a) The subject performs the action
   b) The subject is acted upon or receives the action
   c) The subject performs the action in such a way that emphasizes the subject's participation
   d) The subject performs the action but is unaware of the result of the action

2. A verb in the passive voice:
   a) The subject performs the action
   b) The subject is acted upon or receives the action
   c) The subject performs the action in such a way that emphasizes the subject's participation
   d) The subject performs the action in its own self-interest (reflective action)

3. What is the best explanation of the middle voice in this example: ὁ Ἡρῴδης **ἐνδυσάμενος** ἐσθῆτα βασιλικήν?
   a) Indirect middle
   b) Direct middle (reflexive)
   c) Deponent middle
   d) Permissive middle

4. What is the best explanation of the middle voice in this example: ὁ κύριος ὑμῶν **ἔρχεται**?
   a) Indirect middle
   b) Direct middle (reflexive)
   c) Deponent middle
   d) Permissive middle

5. What is the best explanation of the middle voice in this example: οὐδὲν **ἀπεκρίνατο**?
   a) Indirect middle
   b) Direct middle (reflexive)
   c) Hortatory middle
   d) Permissive middle

6. What is the best explanation of the middle voice in this example: συμβουλεύω (I counsel) σοι ἀγοράσαι παρ' ἐμοῦ . . . ἱμάτια λευκὰ ἵνα **περιβάλῃ** (you should clothe)?
   a) Indirect middle
   b) Direct middle (reflexive)
   c) Deponent middle
   d) Permissive middle

7. What is the best explanation of the middle voice in this example: καὶ **ἐχαρίσατο** αὐτῷ τὸ ὄνομα?
    a) Indirect middle
    b) Direct middle (reflexive)
    c) Deponent middle
    d) Permissive middle

8. What is the best explanation of the middle voice in this example: καθὼς **ἐξελέξατο** ἡμᾶς?
    a) Direct middle (reflexive)
    b) Indirect middle
    c) Hortatory middle
    d) Permissive middle

9. What is the best explanation of the passive voice in this example: γὰρ ἐν ἑνὶ πνεύματι ἡμεῖς πάντες εἰς ἓν σῶμα **ἐβαπτίσθημεν**?
    a) Deponent passive
    b) Simple passive
    c) Passive with an accusative object
    d) Passive with an ultimate agent

10. What is the best explanation of the passive voice in this example: **ἀπεκρίθη** δὲ ὁ χιλίαρχος?
    a) Simple passive
    b) Passive with an accusative object
    c) Deponent passive
    d) Passive with an ultimate agent

ANSWER KEY

1. C, 2. B, 3. B, 4. C, 5. A, 6. B, 7. C, 8. B, 9. B, 10. C

CHAPTER 10

The Indicative Mood

You Should Know

- A mood is the feature of the verb that presents the verbal action or state with reference to its *actuality* or *potentiality*.

- The moods affirm various degrees of certainty. The imperative mood is normally used to address the *volition*, while the optative, subjunctive, and especially indicative address *cognition*.

- Declarative indicative: The indicative is routinely used to present an assertion as a non-contingent (or unqualified) statement.

- Interrogative indicative: The question expects an assertion to be made; it expects a declarative indicative in the answer. By way of contrast, the subjunctive asks a question of moral "oughtness" or obligation, or asks whether something is *possible*.

- Conditional indicative: This is the use of the indicative in the protasis (the "if" clause) of conditional sentences. The conditional element is made explicit with the particle εἰ. First and second-class conditional sentences use the indicative.

- Potential indicative: The indicative is used with verbs of obligation, wish, or desire, followed by an infinitive. Verbs indicating obligation (such as ὀφείλω, δεῖ), wish (e.g., βούλομαι), or desire (e.g., θέλω) are used with an infinitive. This usage is really a subcategory of the declarative indicative.

- Indicative with Ὅτι: There are three broad groups: substantival, epexegetical, and causal.

- What is the best translation for the word θερίζω?
    - I harvest, reap

- What is the best translation for the word φανερόω?
  - I reveal, make known
- What is the best translation for the word θεάομαι?
  - I see, look at
- What is the best translation for the word τελειόω?
  - I complete, bring to an end
- What is the best translation for the word πόθεν?
  - From where, from what source
- What is the best translation for the word μαρτυρία?
  - Testimony, witness, reputation
- What is the best translation for the word ἀληθής?
  - Truthful, righteous
- What is the best translation for the word διαφέρω?
  - I carry through, spread, to be worth more
- What is the best translation for the word οὔπω?
  - Not yet
- What is the best translation for the word πού?
  - Where?

Quiz

1. The action for a verb in the indicative mood is portrayed as:
   a) Certain, asserted
   b) Probable, desired
   c) Possible
   d) Intended

2. What is the best explanation of the indicative mood in this example: εἰ γὰρ ἔγνωσαν, οὐκ ἂν τὸν κύριον τῆς δόξης ἐσταύρωσαν?
   a) Declarative indicative
   b) Interrogative indicative

c) Conditional indicative
d) Potential indicative

3. What is the best explanation of the indicative mood in this example: **ἐξῆλθεν** ὁ σπείρων σπεῖραι (to sow)?
   a) Declarative indicative
   b) Interrogative indicative
   c) Conditional indicative
   d) Potential indicative

4. What is the best explanation of the indicative mood in this example: σὺ **εἶ** ὁ βασιλεὺς τῶν Ἰουδαίων?
   a) Declarative indicative
   b) Interrogative indicative
   c) Conditional indicative
   d) Potential indicative

5. What is the best explanation of the ὅτι clause in this example: καλῶς εἶπας ὅτι ἄνδρα οὐκ ἔχω?
   a) Epexegetical
   b) Direct address
   c) Causal (adverbial)
   d) Interrogative

6. What is the best explanation of the indicative mood in this example: **Βούλομαι** οὖν προσεύχεσθαι τοὺς ἄνδρας?
   a) Declarative indicative
   b) Potential indicative
   c) Interrogative indicative
   d) Conditional indicative

7. What is the best explanation of the indicative mood in this example: εἰ γὰρ **πιστεύομεν** ὅτι Ἰησοῦς ἀπέθανεν . . . ?
   a) Declarative indicative
   b) Interrogative indicative
   c) Potential indicative
   d) Conditional indicative

8. What is the best explanation of the indicative mood in this example: Πάντων δὲ τὸ τέλος ἤγγικεν?

   a) Declarative indicative
   b) Interrogative indicative
   c) Conditional indicative
   d) Potential indicative

9. What is the best explanation of the indicative mood in this example: τί σὺ **λέγεις** περὶ αὐτοῦ?

   a) Declarative indicative
   b) Interrogative indicative
   c) Conditional indicative
   d) Potential indicative

10. What is the best explanation of the ὅτι clause in this example: καὶ εἶπεν πρὸς αὐτούς· τί ὅτι ἐζητεῖτέ με?

    a) Epexegetical
    b) Direct address
    c) Causal (adverbial)
    d) Interrogative

ANSWER KEY
1. A, 2. C, 3. A, 4. B, 5. B, 6. B, 7. D, 8. A, 9. B, 10. A

CHAPTER 11

The Subjunctive Mood

You Should Know

- The subjunctive can be said to represent the verbal action (or state) as uncertain but probable. However, the subjunctive mood encompasses a multitude of nuances.

- Relation to the optative: In the Koine period the optative was dying out. The subjunctive thus, at times, is used for mere possibility or even hypothetical possibility.

- Hortatory subjunctive: used to exhort or command oneself and one's associates; appears in the first-person plural only, typically translated *let us*. . . .

- Deliberative subjunctive: asks either a *real* or *rhetorical* question

- Emphatic negation subjunctive: emphatic negation is indicated by οὐ μή plus the aorist subjunctive or, less frequently, οὐ μή plus the future indicative; the strongest way to negate something in Greek

- Prohibitive subjunctive: used to forbid the occurrence of an action; the structure is usually μή + aorist subjunctive, typically in the second person

- Purpose ἵνα clause (a.k.a. final or telic ἵνα): The most frequent use of ἵνα clauses is to express purpose.

- Result ἵνα clause (a.k.a. consecutive or ecbatic ἵνα): This use of ἵνα + subjunctive expresses the result of the action of the main verb. It indicates a consequence of the verbal action that is not intended. The ἵνα is normally translated "so that," "with the result that."

- What is the best translation for the word γεωργός?
  - Farmer
- What is the best translation for the word κληρονόμος?
  - Heir, beneficiary
- What is the best translation for the word κρύπτω?
  - I hide, keep secret
- What is the best translation for the word καίω?
  - I light, have or keep burning
- What is the best translation for the word καταλύω?
  - I throw down, destroy
- What is the best translation for the word λογίζομαι?
  - I think, believe, consider
- What is the best translation for the word χώρα?
  - Land, district
- What is the best translation for the word κἀκεῖ?
  - And there
- What is the best translation for the word πάσχα?
  - Passover
- What is the best translation for the word ἑορτή?
  - Celebration, festival

Quiz

1. The action for a verb in the subjunctive mood is portrayed as:
    a) Certain, asserted
    b) Probable, desired
    c) Possible
    d) Intended

2. What is the best explanation of the subjunctive mood in this example: μὴ **θαυμάσῃς** ὅτι εἶπόν σοι?
   a) Hortatory subjunctive
   b) Deliberative subjunctive
   c) Emphatic negation subjunctive
   d) Prohibitive subjunctive

3. What is the best explanation of the subjunctive mood in this example: καὶ οὐ μὴ **ἀπόλωνται** εἰς τὸν αἰῶνα?
   a) Hortatory subjunctive
   b) Deliberative subjunctive
   c) Emphatic negation subjunctive
   d) Prohibitive subjunctive

4. What is the best explanation of the subjunctive mood in this example: τί φάγωμεν?
   a) Hortatory subjunctive
   b) Deliberative subjunctive
   c) Emphatic negation subjunctive
   d) Prohibitive subjunctive

4. What is the best explanation of the subjunctive mood in this example: φάγωμεν καὶ πίωμεν?
   a) Hortatory subjunctive
   b) Deliberative subjunctive
   c) Emphatic negation subjunctive
   d) Prohibitive subjunctive

5. What is the best description of "ἵνα plus subjunctive" in this phrase: ταῦτα γράφω ὑμῖν ἵνα μὴ ἁμάρτητε?
   a) Purpose ἵνα clause
   b) Deliberative subjunctive
   c) Indefinite temporal clause
   d) Indefinite relative clause

6. What is the best explanation of the subjunctive mood in this example: μὴ **σκληρύνητε** (make hard) τὰς καρδίας ὑμῶν?

a) Hortatory subjunctive
b) Deliberative subjunctive
c) Emphatic negation subjunctive
d) Prohibitive subjunctive

7. What is the best explanation of the subjunctive mood in this example: καὶ ἐπιθυμίαν σαρκὸς οὐ μὴ **τελέσητε**?

a) Hortatory subjunctive
b) Deliberative subjunctive
c) Emphatic negation subjunctive
d) Prohibitive subjunctive

8. What is the best explanation of the two subjunctive moods in this example: **ἀποθώμεθα** οὖν τὰ ἔργα τοῦ σκότους, **ἐνδυσώμεθα** δὲ τὰ ὅπλα (armor) τοῦ φωτός?

a) Hortatory subjunctive
b) Deliberative subjunctive
c) Emphatic negation subjunctive
d) Prohibitive subjunctive

9. What is the best description of "ἵνα plus subjunctive" in this phrase: τίς ἥμαρτεν . . . ἵνα τυφλὸς **γεννηθῇ**?

a) Purpose ἵνα clause
b) Deliberative subjunctive
c) Result ἵνα clause
d) Indefinite relative clause

ANSWER KEY

1. B, 2. D, 3. C, 4. B, 5. A, 6. A, 7. D, 8. C, 9. A, 10. C

CHAPTER 12

The Optative and Imperative Moods

You Should Know

- The optative is the mood used when a speaker wishes to portray an action as possible. There are less than 70 optatives in the entire NT.

- Voluntative optative: The use of the optative in an independent clause to express an *obtainable wish* or a *prayer*. It is frequently an appeal to the will, in particular when used in prayers.

- Oblique optative: The optative may be used in indirect questions after a secondary tense. The optative substitutes for an indicative or subjunctive of the direct question. This occurs about a dozen times, only in Luke's writings.

- The imperative mood is the mood of intention. It is the mood furthest removed from certainty. The imperative moves in the realm of *volition* and *possibility*.

- Imperative mood command: The imperative is most commonly used for commands, five times more common than the prohibitive imperative. With the aorist, the force generally is to command the action as a whole. With the present, the force generally is to command the action as an ongoing process. The third person imperative is normally translated *Let him do*, etc.

- Imperative mood prohibition: The imperative is commonly used to forbid an action. The negative particle μή (or a cognate) is used before the imperative to turn a command into a prohibition.

- Imperative mood request: The imperative is often used to express a request when the speaker is addressing a superior.

- What is the best translation for the word ὑποτάσσω?
  - I subject, bring into subjugation
- What is the best translation for the word φεύγω?
  - I flee, escape
- What is the best translation for the word ἐγγίζω?
  - I draw near
- What is the best translation for the word κελεύω?
  - I command, order, urge
- What is the best translation for the word ἰσχυρός?
  - Strong, violent
- What is the best translation for the word τράπεζα?
  - Table, meal
- What is the best translation for the word σκάνδαλον?
  - Trap, enticement
- What is the best translation for the word πλοῦτος?
  - Riches, wealth
- What is the best translation for the word θαυμάζω?
  - I wonder, marvel, admire
- What is the best translation for the word ὑπακούω?
  - I obey, follow

Quiz

1. The action for a verb in the imperative mood is portrayed as:
    a) Certain, asserted
    b) Probable, desired
    c) Possible
    d) Intended

2. The action for a verb in the optative mood is portrayed as:
    a) Certain, asserted
    b) Probable, desired
    c) Possible
    d) Intended

3. What is the best explanation of the imperative mood in this example: ἐλθέτω ἡ βασιλεία σου?
    a) Voluntative optative
    b) Imperative of command
    c) Imperative of prohibition
    d) Imperative of request

4. What is the best explanation of the imperative mood in this example: μὴ φοβοῦ?
    a) Voluntative optative
    b) Imperative of command
    c) Imperative of prohibition
    d) Imperative of request

5. What is the best explanation of the imperative mood in this example: ἀκολούθει μοι?
    a) Voluntative optative
    b) Imperative of command
    c) Imperative of prohibition
    d) Imperative of request

6. What is the best explanation of the imperative mood in this example: δῴη ἔλεος ὁ κύριος τῷ Ὀνησιφόρου οἴκῳ?
    a) Voluntative optative
    b) Imperative of command
    c) Imperative of prohibition
    d) Imperative of request

7. What is the best explanation of the imperative mood in this example: χαρίσασθέ μοι τὴν ἀδικίαν ταύτην?
    a) Voluntative optative
    b) Imperative of command

c) Imperative of prohibition
d) Imperative of request

8. What is the best explanation of the imperative mood in this example: Μὴ **ἀγαπᾶτε** τὸν κόσμον μηδὲ τὰ ἐν τῷ κόσμῳ?

   a) Voluntative optative
   b) Imperative of command
   c) Imperative of prohibition
   d) Imperative of request

9. What is the best explanation of the imperative mood in this example: Ἑαυτοὺς **πειράζετε** εἰ ἐστὲ ἐν τῇ πίστει?

   a) Voluntative optative
   b) Imperative of command
   c) Imperative of prohibition
   d) Imperative of request

10. What is the best explanation of the imperative mood in this example: χάρις ὑμῖν καὶ εἰρήνη **πληθυνθείη**?

    a) Imperative of command
    b) Imperative of prohibition
    c) Voluntative optative
    d) Oblique optative

ANSWER KEY

1. D, 2. C, 3. D, 4. C, 5. B, 6. A, 7. D, 8. C, 9. B, 10. C

CHAPTER 13

The Present Tense

You Should Know

- In general, tense in Greek involves two elements: aspect (kind of action, complete or incomplete) and time. Aspect is *the primary value of tense in Greek* and time is secondary, if involved at all.

- Three kinds of time: past, present, future. In the indicative mood, time is *clearly* involved. For participles, time is *often* involved, although it is relative (or dependent) on the time of the main verb. In the subjunctive, optative, imperative, infinitive, except in indirect discourse, time is *not involved*.

- Definition of aspect: Verbal aspect is, in general, the portrayal of the action (or state) as to its *progress*, *results*, or *simple occurrence*.

- Instantaneous present: The present tense may be used to indicate that an action is completed at the moment of speaking.

- Progressive present: The present tense may be used to describe a scene in progress, especially in narrative literature.

- Iterative present: The present tense may be used to describe an event that repeatedly happens.

- Customary present: The customary present is used to signal either an action that *regularly occurs* or an *ongoing state*.

- Gnomic present: The present tense may be used to make a statement of a general, timeless fact.

- Historical present: The historical present is used frequently in narrative literature to describe a past event. Usually in English we do not mix past and present in the same sentence.

- Futuristic present: The present tense may be used to describe a future event, though it typically adds the connotations of immediacy and certainty.
- What is the best translation for the word ἐπιγινώσκω?
  - I know, perceive
- What is the best translation for the word καθίζω?
  - I cause to sit down, sit
- What is the best translation for the word γρηγορέω?
  - I am watchful, I am on alert
- What is the best translation for the word ἀσθενής?
  - Sick, ill, weak
- What is the best translation for the word ποτήριον?
  - Cup, drinking vessel
- What is the best translation for the word τελώνης?
  - Tax collector
- What is the best translation for the word ἁμαρτωλός?
  - Sinner
- What is the best translation for the word νηστεύω?
  - I fast
- What is the best translation for the word κακῶς?
  - Bad, badly, severely
- What is the best translation for the word παρέρχομαι?
  - I go or pass by

Quiz

1. The present tense portrays an event by focusing on:
    a) Its development or progress usually in present time
    b) Its development or progress usually in past time

c) The whole event from the outside, usually in past time
d) An accomplished event in the past with results in present time

2. What is the best explanation of the present tense in this example: πολλάκις γὰρ **πίπτει** εἰς τὸ πῦρ?

   a) Progressive present
   b) Iterative present
   c) Futuristic present
   d) Historical present

3. What is the best explanation of the present tense in this example: ὅτι πάντες **ζητοῦσίν** σε?

   a) Progressive present
   b) Iterative present
   c) Gnomic present
   d) Historical present

4. What is the best explanation of the present tense in this example: ἱλαρὸν γὰρ δότην **ἀγαπᾷ** ὁ θεός?

   a) Progressive present
   b) Iterative present
   c) Gnomic present
   d) Historical present

5. What is the best explanation of the present tenses in this example: καὶ **ἔρχεται** πρὸς τοὺς μαθητὰς καὶ **εὑρίσκει** αὐτοὺς καθεύδοντας?

   a) Progressive present
   b) Futuristic present
   c) Gnomic present
   d) Historical present

6. What is the best explanation of the present tenses in this example: ναί, **ἔρχομαι** ταχύ?

   a) Progressive present
   b) Futuristic present
   c) Gnomic present
   d) Historical present

7. What is the best explanation of the present tense in this example: οὐδεὶς γὰρ δύναται ταῦτα τὰ σημεῖα ποιεῖν ἃ σὺ **ποιεῖς** . . .?
   a) Progressive present
   b) Futuristic present
   c) Iterative present
   d) Historical present

8. What is the best explanation of the present tense in this example: **νηστεύω** δὶς τοῦ σαββάτου?
   a) Customary present
   b) Iterative present
   c) Gnomic present
   d) Historical present

9. What is the best explanation of the present tense in this example: πᾶς ἄνθρωπος πρῶτον τὸν καλὸν οἶνον **τίθησιν**?
   a) Gnomic present
   b) Progressive present
   c) Iterative present
   d) Historical present

10. What is the best explanation of the present tenses in this example: καὶ ἀπήγγειλαν αὐτῷ πάντα ὅσα ἐποίησαν καὶ ὅσα ἐδίδαξαν καὶ **λέγει** αὐτοῖς?
    a) Progressive present
    b) Historical present
    c) Futuristic present
    d) Gnomic present

ANSWER KEY
1. A, 2. B, 3. A, 4. C, 5. D, 6. B, 7. C, 8. A, 9. A, 10. B

CHAPTER 14

The Imperfect Tense

You Should Know

- In general, tense in Greek involves two elements: aspect (kind of action, complete or incomplete) and time. Aspect is *the primary value of tense in Greek* and time is secondary, if involved at all.

- Like the present tense, the imperfect displays an *internal aspect*. With reference to time, the imperfect is *almost always past*.

- Progressive (descriptive) imperfect: used to describe an action or state that is in progress in past time from the viewpoint of the speaker

- Ingressive imperfect: used to stress the beginning of an action, with the implication that it continued for some time

- The ingressive imperfect, in contrast to the ingressive aorist, stresses beginning, but *implies that the action continues*. The ingressive aorist stresses beginning, but *does not imply that the action continues*.

- Iterative imperfect: used for repeated action in past time; key words — *kept on doing, going; repeatedly, continuously doing*

- Customary imperfect: used to indicate a regularly recurring activity in past time (habitual) or a state that continued for some time (general)

- What is the best translation for the word διώκω?
  - I persecute, pursue

- What is the best translation for the word προσευχή?
  - Prayer, intercession

- What is the best translation for the word βαστάζω?
  - I pick up, take up, carry
- What is the best translation for the word εἰσπορεύομαι?
  - I go into, enter
- What is the best translation for the word ἐπιγινώσκω?
  - I know, understand
- What is the best translation for the word ἀργύριον?
  - Silver
- What is the best translation for the word χρυσίον?
  - Gold
- What is the best translation for the word ἐργάζομαι?
  - I work
- What is the best translation for the word ἄρτι?
  - Now
- What is the best translation for the word κοιλία?
  - Belly, stomach, womb

Quiz

1. The imperfect tense portrays an event by focusing on:
   a) Its development or progress usually in present time
   a) Its development or progress usually in past time
   b) The whole event from the outside, usually in past time
   c) An accomplished event in the past with results in present time

2. What is the best explanation of the imperfect tense in this example: Καὶ **ἐπορεύοντο** οἱ γονεῖς αὐτοῦ κατ' ἔτος εἰς Ἰερουσαλήμ?
   a) Progressive imperfect
   b) Ingressive imperfect

c) Iterative imperfect
d) Customary imperfect

3. What is the best explanation of the imperfect tense in this example: πεσὼν ἐπὶ τῆς γῆς **ἐκυλίετο** (rolling)?

a) Progressive imperfect
b) Ingressive imperfect
c) Iterative imperfect
d) Customary imperfect

4. What is the best explanation of the imperfect tense in this example: αὐτὸς δὲ **ἐκάθευδεν**?

a) Progressive imperfect
b) Ingressive imperfect
c) Iterative imperfect
d) Customary imperfect

5. What is the best explanation of the imperfect tense in this example: καθ' ἡμέραν (daily) ἐν τῷ ἱερῷ **ἐκαθεζόμην** (I was sitting) διδάσκων?

a) Progressive imperfect
b) Ingressive imperfect
c) Iterative imperfect
d) Customary imperfect

6. What is the best explanation of the imperfect tense in this example: καὶ **ἔλεγον**·χαῖρε (hail!) ὁ βασιλεὺς τῶν Ἰουδαίων?

a) Progressive imperfect
b) Ingressive imperfect
c) Iterative imperfect
d) Customary imperfect

7. What is the best explanation of the imperfect tense in this example: Βαρναβᾶς δὲ **ἐβούλετο** συμπαραλαβεῖν (to take along with) καὶ τὸν Ἰωάννην?

a) Progressive imperfect
b) Ingressive imperfect
c) Conative imperfect
d) Customary imperfect

8. What is the best explanation of the imperfect tense in this example: καὶ ἀνοίξας τὸ στόμα αὐτοῦ **ἐδίδασκεν** αὐτοὺς λέγων . . .?

   a) Progressive imperfect
   b) Ingressive imperfect
   c) Iterative imperfect
   d) Customary imperfect

9. Why is the imperfect tense used in this example: ὁ δὲ κύριος προσετίθει τοὺς σῳζομένους καθ' ἡμέραν?

   a) Because the Lord was beginning to add to those being saved
   b) Because the Lord was continually adding to those being saved daily
   c) Because the Lord habitually added to the ones being saved
   d) Because the root προστίθημι is deponent

ANSWER KEY

1. B, 2. D, 3. B, 4. A, 5. D, 6. C, 7. A, 8. B, 9. B

CHAPTER 15

The Aorist and Future Tenses

You Should Know

- The aorist tense "presents an occurrence in summary, viewed as a whole from the outside, without regard for the internal make-up of the occurrence." Think of the aorist as taking a *snapshot of the action* while the imperfect (like the present) takes a motion picture, portraying the action as it unfolds.

- In the indicative, the aorist usually indicates past time with reference to the time of speaking. Aorist participles usually suggest antecedent time to that of the main verb.

- Constative aorist: It describes the action in summary fashion, without focusing on the beginning or end of the action specifically. It places the stress on the fact of the occurrence, not its nature.

- Ingressive aorist: used to stress the beginning of an action or the entrance into a state; unlike the ingressive imperfect, there is no implication that the action continues; usually with stative verbs.

- Consummative aorist: The aorist is often used to stress the cessation of an act or state

- Gnomic aorist: The aorist indicative is occasionally used to present a timeless, general fact.

- With reference to aspect, the future seems to offer an external portrayal, something of a temporal counterpart to the aorist indicative. With reference to time, the future tense is always future from the speaker's

- Predictive future: The future tense may indicate that something will take place or come to pass. The portrayal is external, summarizing the action: "it will happen."

- What is the best translation for the word ἀνέχω?
  - I endure, bear up with

- What is the best translation for the word ἐκλεκτός?
  - Chosen, elect, choice

- What is the best translation for the word κλαίω?
  - I weep, cry

- What is the best translation for the word ἐχθρός?
  - Hostile, hated, enemy

- What is the best translation for the word κρύπτω?
  - I hide, keep secret

- What is the best translation for the word μηκέτι?
  - No longer

- What is the best translation for the word παραχρῆμα?
  - At once, immediately

- What is the best translation for the word ἥκω?
  - I have come, am present

- What is the best translation for the word ξηραίνω?
  - I wither, become dry

- What is the best translation for the word καταλείπω?
  - I leave (behind), leave

Quiz

1. The aorist tense portrays an event by focusing on:
    a) Its development or progress usually in present time
    b) Its development or progress usually in past time

c) The whole event from the outside, usually in past time
d) An accomplished event in the past with results in present time

2. What is the best explanation of the aorist tenses in this example: ἐκτείνας τὴν χεῖρα **ἥψατο** αὐτοῦ?

a) Constative aorist
b) Ingressive aorist
c) Consummative aorist
d) Proleptic aorist

3. What is the best explanation of the aorist tense in this example: **ἠκολούθησαν** αὐτῷ δύο τυφλοί?

a) Constative aorist
b) Ingressive aorist
c) Consummative aorist
d) Proleptic aorist

4. What is the best explanation of the aorist tense in this example: **ἐνίκησεν** ὁ λέων ὁ ἐκ τῆς φυλῆς Ἰούδα?

a) Constative aorist
b) Ingressive aorist
c) Consummative aorist
d) Proleptic aorist

5. What is the best explanation of the aorist tense in this example: ὁ δὲ βασιλεὺς **ὠργίσθη**?

a) Constative aorist
b) Ingressive aorist
c) Consummative aorist
d) Proleptic aorist

6. What is the best explanation of the aorist tenses in this example: ὅτι ἐπὶ τοῦτο **ἀπεστάλην**?

a) Constative aorist
b) Ingressive aorist
c) Consummative aorist
d) Proleptic aorist

7. What is the best explanation of the aorist tenses in this example: ὃς ἐγένετο νεκρὸς καὶ ἔζησεν?

   a) Constative aorist
   b) Ingressive aorist
   c) Consummative aorist
   d) Proleptic aorist

8. What is the best explanation of the aorist tense in this example: ἐπείσθησαν δὲ αὐτῷ?

   a) Constative aorist
   b) Ingressive aorist
   c) Consummative aorist
   d) Proleptic aorist

9. What is the best explanation of the future tense in this example: καὶ οἱ νεκροὶ ἐν Χριστῷ ἀναστήσονται πρῶτον?

   a) Imperatival future
   b) Predictive future
   c) Deliberative future
   d) Future for present action

10. Why did the writer use an aorist tense verb in this example in Rev 20:4: καὶ ἐβασίλευσαν μετὰ τοῦ Χριστοῦ . . . ?

    a) In order to emphasize the cessation of the action
    b) In order to describe the action as a timeless truth
    c) In order to stress the beginning of the action
    d) In order to stress the completeness of the action

ANSWER KEY

1. C, 2. A, 3. B, 4. C, 5. B, 6. A, 7. B, 8. C, 9. B, 10. C

CHAPTER 16

The Perfect and Pluperfect Tenses

You Should Know

- The perfect and pluperfect tenses both speak of an event accomplished in the past (in the indicative mood) with results existing afterwards. The perfect speaks of results existing in the present, the pluperfect speaks of results existing in the past.

- The aspect of the perfect and pluperfect is sometimes called *stative*, *resultative*, *completed*, or *perfective-stative*. The perfect and pluperfect tenses both speak of an event accomplished in the past (in the indicative mood) with results existing afterwards.

- Intensive perfect: used to emphasize the results or present state produced by a past action. The English present tense is usually best.

- Extensive perfect: used to emphasize the completed action of a past action or process from which a present state emerges; usually translated as an English perfect ("has been")

- Perfect with present force: Certain verbs occur frequently (or exclusively) in the perfect tense without the usual aspectual significance (e.g., οἶδα).

- The pluperfect occurs only in the indicative mood. It may be said that the pluperfect combines the aspects of the aorist (for the event) and the imperfect (for the results).

- Intensive pluperfect: used of the pluperfect; places the emphasis on the results that existed in past time

- Extensive pluperfect: used to emphasize the completion of an action in past time, without focusing as much on the existing results

- Pluperfect with past force: Certain verbs occur frequently (or exclusively) in the perfect and pluperfect tenses without the usual aspectual significance (e.g., οἶδα, ᾔδειν).
- What is the best translation for the word φίλος?
  - Beloved, friend (subst.)
- What is the best translation for the word κοιμάω?
  - I sleep, die
- What is the best translation for the word τέσσαρες?
  - Four
- What is the best translation for the word μνημεῖον?
  - Memorial, grave
- What is the best translation for the word καθέζομαι?
  - I sit, remain
- What is the best translation for the word λύω?
  - I loose, destroy
- What is the best translation for the word πάρειμι?
  - I am present, have come
- What is the best translation for the word δέω?
  - I bind, tie
- What is the best translation for the word φωνέω?
  - I call or cry out
- What is the best translation for the word πάντοτε?
  - Always, at all times

Quiz

1. The perfect tense portrays an event by focusing on:
    a) Its development or progress usually in present time
    b) Its development or progress usually in past time

c) The whole event from the outside, usually in past time

d) An accomplished event in the past with results in present time

2. What is the best explanation of the perfect tense in this example: ἡ ἀγάπη τοῦ θεοῦ **ἐκκέχυται** (has been poured out) ἐν ταῖς καρδίαις ἡμῶν?

 a) Intensive perfect
 b) Extensive perfect
 c) Perfect with a present force
 d) Pluperfect with a simple past force

3. What is the best explanation of the perfect tense in this example: τὰς ἐντολὰς **οἶδας**?

 a) Intensive perfect
 b) Extensive perfect
 c) Perfect with a present force
 d) Pluperfect with a simple past force

4. What is the best explanation of the pluperfect tense in this example: ὅτι **ᾔδεισαν** αὐτόν?

 a) Intensive perfect
 b) Extensive perfect
 c) Intensive pluperfect
 d) Pluperfect with a simple past force

5. What is the best explanation of the perfect tense in this example: ἤδη γὰρ **συνετέθειντο** (had agreed) οἱ Ἰουδαῖοι?

 a) Intensive perfect
 b) Extensive perfect
 c) Perfect with a present force
 d) Extensive pluperfect

6. What is the best explanation of the perfect tense in this example: ἄνθρωπε, **ἀφέωνταί** σοι αἱ ἁμαρτίαι σου?

 a) Extensive perfect
 b) Perfect with a present force
 c) Pluperfect with a simple past force
 d) Intensive perfect

7. What is the best explanation of the perfect tense in this example: ῥαββί, **οἴδαμεν** ὅτι ἀπὸ θεοῦ ἐλήλυθας διδάσκαλος?
   a) Intensive perfect
   b) Extensive perfect
   c) Perfect with a present force
   d) Pluperfect with a simple past force

8. What is the best explanation of the pluperfect tense in this example: ἄνδρες δύο **παρειστήκεισαν** αὐτοῖς?
   a) Intensive perfect
   b) Extensive perfect
   c) Intensive pluperfect
   d) Pluperfect with a simple past force

9. What is the best explanation of the perfect tense in this example: καὶ ἡμεῖς τεθεάμεθα καὶ μαρτυροῦμεν?
   a) Extensive perfect
   b) Perfect with a present force
   c) Pluperfect with a simple past force
   d) Intensive perfect

ANSWER KEY
1. D, 2. B, 3. C, 4. D, 5. D, 6. D, 7. C, 8. D, 9. D

CHAPTER 17

The Infinitive

You Should Know

- The infinitive is an indeclinable verbal noun. As such it participates in some of the features of the verb and some of the noun. Like a verb, the infinitive has tense and voice, but not person or mood. Like a noun, the infinitive can have many of the case functions that an ordinary noun can have. It can function as the object of a preposition, be anarthrous and articular, and be modified by an adjective. When used with an infinitive, the *neuter article* has no other significance than a formal attachment. The infinitive often occurs after prepositions. When it does so, the infinitive *is always articular*.

- Purpose: The infinitive is used to indicate the purpose or goal of the action or state of its controlling verb.

- Result: The infinitive of result indicates the outcome produced by the controlling verb. The infinitive of purpose puts an emphasis on intention. The infinitive of result puts an emphasis on effect.

- Time: This use of the infinitive indicates a temporal relationship between its action and the action of the controlling verb. It answers the question, "When?" (I.e., when did the infinitive action happen relative to the main verb?)

- Cause: The causal infinitive indicates the reason for the action of the controlling verb. In this respect, it answers the question "Why?"

- Complementary: The infinitive is frequently used with "helper" verbs to complete their thought. Such verbs rarely occur without the infinitive.

- Subject: An infinitive or an infinitive phrase frequently functions as the subject of a finite verb. The infinitive may or may not have the article.

- Indirect discourse: the use of the infinitive (or infinitive phrase) after a verb of *perception or communication*

- The appositional infinitive *defines* the noun or adjective to which it is related. The epexegetical infinitive *explains* the noun or adjective to which it is related.

- What is the best translation for the word παύω?
    - I stop, cease

- What is the best translation for the word ἔρημος?
    - Desert, wilderness

- What is the best translation for the word ῥίζα?
    - Root, descendant

- What is the best translation for the word διδαχή?
    - Instruction, teaching

- What is the best translation for the word ἀνατέλλω?
    - I rise, cause to rise

- What is the best translation for the word παραλαμβάνω?
    - I receive, take

- What is the best translation for the word ἀπέχω?
    - I abstain, refrain from

- What is the best translation for the word τιμή?
    - Honor, respect

- What is the best translation for the word χρεία?
    - Need, what should be

- What is the best translation for the word πάθος?
    - Passion

Quiz

1. When the infinitive is used with a definite article, it is called:
   a) A deponent infinitive
   b) An anarthrous infinitive
   c) An articular infinitive
   d) A complementary infinitive

2. When the infinitive is used to complete the meaning of another verb, it is called:
   a) A complementary infinitive
   b) An anarthrous infinitive
   c) A deponent infinitive
   d) An articular infinitive

3. What is the use of the following adverbial infinitive: ἐν τῷ **σπείρειν** αὐτόν?
   a) Result
   b) Purpose
   c) Time
   d) Cause

4. What is the use of the following adverbial infinitive: ὥστε **βυθίζεσθαι** (to sink) αὐτά?
   a) Result
   b) Purpose
   c) Time
   d) Cause

5. What is the use of the following substantival infinitive: ἐλευθέρα ἐστὶν ᾧ θέλει **γαμηθῆναι** (to be married)?
   a) Epexegetical
   b) Appositional
   c) Subject
   d) Direct discourse

6. What is the use of the following substantival infinitives: τὸ **ζῆν** (to live) Χριστὸς καὶ τὸ **ἀποθανεῖν** κέρδος?

a) Epexegetical
b) Appositional
c) Subject
d) Direct discourse

7. What is the use of the following adverbial infinitive: καὶ εὐθέως ἐξανέτειλεν **διὰ τὸ μὴ ἔχειν** βάθος γῆς?

a) Result
b) Purpose
c) Time
d) Cause

8. What is the use of the following adverbial infinitive: ἐνδύσασθε τὴν πανοπλίαν (armor) τοῦ θεοῦ **πρὸς τὸ δύνασθαι** ὑμᾶς στῆναι?

a) Result
b) Purpose
c) Time
d) Cause

9. What is the use of the following adverbial infinitive: καὶ ἐὰν ἔχω πᾶσαν τὴν πίστιν **ὥστε** ὄρη (mountains) **μεθιστάναι** (to move)?

a) Result
b) Purpose
c) Time
d) Cause

10. What is the use of the following substantival infinitive: ὅτι ἔχει πίστιν **τοῦ σωθῆναι**?

a) Epexegetical
b) Appositional
c) Subject
d) Direct discourse

ANSWER KEY

1. C, 2. A, 3. C, 4. A, 5. A, 6. C, 7. D, 8. B, 9. A, 10. A

CHAPTER 18

The Participle (Part 1)

You Should Know

- The participle is a declinable verbal adjective. It derives from its verbal nature tense and voice; from its adjectival nature, gender, number, and case.

- The tenses behave just as they do in the indicative. The only *difference* is that now the *point of reference is the controlling verb*, not the speaker.

- The present participle is used for contemporaneous time. The aorist participle usually denotes antecedent time, but sometimes may indicate contemporaneous time. The perfect participle indicates antecedent time. The future participle denotes subsequent time.

- The participle's aspect still functions for the most part like its indicative counterparts.

- Many substantival participles in the NT are used in generic utterances so that kind of action is not important.

- The tenses behave just as they do in the indicative. The only *difference* is that now the point of reference is the controlling verb, not the speaker.

- Attributive participles: The participle functions like an attributive adjective.

- Predicate participles: The participle functions like a predicate adjective. The predicate participle never has the article (only the attributive and substantival participles do).

- Substantival (independent): This is the independent use of the adjectival participle, not related to a noun.

- What is the best translation for the word ἀνάκειμαι?
  - I recline, dine
- What is the best translation for the word ἡγέομαι?
  - I think, consider, regard
- What is the best translation for the word ταπεινόω?
  - I lower, humble
- What is the best translation for the word χαρίζομαι?
  - I give graciously
- What is the best translation for the word παράπτωμα?
  - Offense, sin
- What is the best translation for the word ὀργή?
  - Anger, wrath, indignation
- What is the best translation for the word ἔλεος?
  - Mercy, compassion
- What is the best translation for the word πλοῦτος?
  - Wealth, abundance
- What is the best translation for the word κτίζω?
  - I create, make
- What is the best translation for the word ἐπιθυμία?
  - Desire, longing, craving

Quiz

1. With respect to time, an aorist participle denotes:
    a) Subsequent time to the main verb
    b) Antecedent time to the main verb
    c) Contemporaneous time to the main verb
    d) The participle has no time function at all

2. With respect to time, a present participle denotes:
   a) Subsequent time to the main verb
   b) Antecedent time to the main verb
   c) Contemporaneous time to the main verb
   d) The participle has no time function at all

3. What is the best explanation of the participle in this example: τὸ ὕδωρ τὸ ζῶν?
   a) Adjectival participle
   b) Substantival participle
   c) Dependent verbal participle
   d) Genitive absolute

4. What is the best explanation of the participle in this example: πᾶς ὁ πιστεύων?
   a) Adjectival participle
   b) Substantival participle
   c) Dependent verbal participle
   d) Genitive absolute

5. The best translation of a substantival participle is:
   a) "Because of . . ."
   b) "The one who . . ."
   c) "Although . . ."
   d) "If . . ."

6. What is the best explanation of the participle in this example: Ζῶν γὰρ ὁ λόγος τοῦ θεοῦ?
   a) Adjectival, attributive participle
   b) Substantival participle
   c) Adjectival, predicate participle
   d) Genitive absolute

7. What is the best explanation of the participle in this example: ὁ λαὸς **ὁ καθήμενος** ἐν σκότει?
   a) Adjectival participle
   b) Adjectival, predicate participle

c) Dependent verbal participle
d) Adjectival, attributive participle

8. What is the best explanation of the participle in this example: πολλοὶ δὲ **τῶν ἀκουσάντων** τὸν λόγον ἐπίστευσαν?

   a) Adjectival, attributive participle
   b) Substantival participle
   c) Adjectival, predicate participle
   d) Genitive absolute

9. What is the best explanation of the participle in this example: ὁ Ἰησοῦς εἶπεν ὦ γενεὰ ἄπιστος καὶ **διεστραμμένη**?

   a) Adjectival participle
   b) Substantival participle
   c) Dependent verbal participle
   d) Genitive absolute

10. What is the best explanation of the participle in this example: ἰδοὺ θεωρῶ τοὺς οὐρανοὺς **διηνοιγμένους** (being opened)?

    a) Adjectival, predicate participle
    b) Substantival participle
    c) Dependent verbal participle
    d) Periphrastic participle

ANSWER KEY

1. B, 2. C, 3. A, 4. B, 5. B, 6. C, 7. D, 8. B, 9. A, 10. A

CHAPTER 19

The Participle (Part 2)

You Should Know

- Temporal: In relation to its controlling verb, the temporal participle answers the question, *When*?

- Manner: The participle indicates the manner in which the action of the finite verb is carried out. The participle of manner refers to the *emotion* (or sometimes *attitude*) that accompanies the main verb.

- Means: This participle indicates the means by which the action of a finite verb is accomplished. This means may be physical or mental. Supply *by* or *by means of* before the participle in translation. The participle of means could be called an *epexegetical* participle in that it defines or explains the action of the controlling verb.

- Cause: The causal participle indicates the cause or reason or ground of the action of the finite verb. This participle answers the question, *Why*? The thought of this participle can be brought out by *since* or *because*. The causal participle normally precedes the verb it modifies.

- Condition: This participle implies a condition on which the fulfillment of the idea indicated by the main verb depends. Its force can be introduced by *if* in translation. This participle is almost always equivalent to the third-class condition rather than first class. It usually represents some sense of uncertainty.

- Concession: The concessive participle implies that the state or action of the main verb is true in spite of the state or action of the participle. Its force is usually best translated with *although*. This is semantically the opposite of the causal participle, but structurally identical. There are often particles that help to make the concessive idea more obvious (such as καίπερ, καίτοιγε).

- Purpose (telic): The participle of purpose indicates the purpose of the action of the finite verb. Unlike other participles, a simple "-ing" flavor will miss the point. Almost always this use should usually be translated like an English *infinitive*, or add the phrase *with the purpose of* before the participle in translation. Perfect participles *are never* purpose, future adverbial participles *always* are purpose.

- Result: The participle of result is used to indicate the actual outcome or result of the action of the main verb. The result participle will be a present tense participle and will follow (in word order) the main verb. Use the phrase "with the result of" before the participle in translation.

- Participle of attendant circumstance: The attendant circumstance participle is used to communicate an action that, in some sense, is coordinate with the finite verb. In this respect it is not dependent, for it is translated like a verb. Yet it is still dependent semantically, because it cannot exist without the main verb.

- Genitive absolute: Structurally, the genitive absolute consists of the following: a noun or pronoun in the genitive case (though this is sometimes absent); a genitive anarthrous participle (always); the entire construction at the front of a sentence (usually). Semantically, there are again three items to notice, once the structure has been identified: This construction is unconnected with the rest of the sentence. The participle is always adverbial (circumstantial) or, at least, dependent-verbal.

- What is the best translation for the word ἀγοράζω?
  – I buy, acquire

- What is the best translation for the word γένος?
  – Descendent, family, nation

- What is the best translation for the word ἀγνοέω?
  – I do not know, do not understand

- What is the best translation for the word ξύλον?
  - Wood

- What is the best translation for the word αἰτία?
  - Cause, reason

- What is the best translation for the word ἱκανός?
  - Sufficient, large, many

- What is the best translation for the word χώρα?
  - Land, region, country

- What is the best translation for the word ἐπίσταμαι?
  - I know, understand

- What is the best translation for the word διαλέγομαι?
  - I converse, discuss

- What is the best translation for the word ἀνάγκη?
  - Necessity

Quiz

1. What is the best description of the use of the participle in the following phrase: ἐστε σεσῳσμένοι?
   a) Attendant circumstance
   b) Periphrastic participle
   c) Genitive absolute
   d) Adverbial participle of result

2. What is the best description of the use of the participle in the following phrase: Ταῦτα αὐτοῦ λαλοῦντος?
   a) Attendant circumstance
   b) Periphrastic participle
   c) Genitive absolute
   d) Adverbial participle of result

3. What is the best explanation of the participle in this example: ἀπῆλθεν **λυπούμενος**?

   a) Temporal
   b) Manner
   c) Means
   d) Cause

4. What is the best explanation of the participle in this example: ἵνα τοὺς δύο κτίσῃ ἐν αὐτῷ εἰς ἕνα καινὸν ἄνθρωπον **ποιῶν** εἰρήνην?

   a) Condition
   b) Concession
   c) Temporal
   d) Result

5. What is the best explanation of the participle in this example: θερίσομεν μὴ **ἐκλυόμενοι** (lose heart)?

   a) Condition
   b) Concession
   c) Purpose (telic)
   d) Result

6. What is the best explanation of the participle in this example: τοῦτο δὲ ἔλεγεν **σημαίνων** (signifying) ποίῳ θανάτῳ ἤμελλεν ἀποθνῄσκειν?

   a) Condition
   b) Concession
   c) Purpose (telic)
   d) Result

7. What is the best explanation of the participle in this example: ἥμαρτον **παραδοὺς** αἷμα ἀθῷον (innocent blood)?

   a) Temporal
   b) Manner
   c) Means
   d) Cause

8. What is the best explanation of the participle in this example: ὑμᾶς **ὄντας** νεκρούς?

a) Condition
b) Concession
c) Purpose (telic)
d) Result

9. What is the best explanation of the participle in this example: καὶ ἠγαλλιάσατο πανοικεὶ **πεπιστευκὼς** τῷ θεῷ?

   a) Temporal
   b) Manner
   c) Means
   d) Cause

10. What is the best explanation of the participle in this example: Καὶ **προβὰς** (going ahead) ὀλίγον εἶδεν Ἰάκωβον τὸν τοῦ Ζεβεδαίου?

    a) Temporal
    b) Manner
    c) Means
    d) Cause

ANSWER KEY
1. B, 2. C, 3. B, 4. D, 5. A, 6. C, 7. C, 8. B, 9. D, 10. A

CHAPTER 20

Conditional Sentences

You Should Know

- There are over 600 formal conditional sentences in the New Testament. Some of the great themes of biblical theology cannot be properly understood apart from a correct understanding of conditions.

- Structurally, a conditional sentence has two parts: An "if" part and a "then" part. "IF" = protasis; "THEN" = apodosis

- The conditional element: Only the protasis is the conditional element. That is, the contingency lies with the "if," not the "then."

- Relation to reality: The portrayal is never a complete picture of reality. This does not necessarily mean that it is incorrect, but neither is the portrayal necessarily correct either.

- Converse of the condition (semantically): The converse of "If A, then B" is "If B, then A." The converse of a condition *is not necessarily true*.

- Reverse of the condition (semantically): The reverse of the condition, "If A happens, B happens" is "If A does not happen, B (still) happens." The reverse of the condition is *not necessarily false*.

- First class condition (assumed true for argument's sake): not "since"! In apparently only 37% of the instances is there a correspondence to reality. "Assumed true for the sake of argument" lends itself to the notion of *presentation* of reality.

- Second class condition (contrary to fact): the assumption of an untruth (for the sake of argument). In the protasis the structure is εἰ + indicative mood with a secondary tense (aorist or imperfect usually). The apodosis usually has ἄν and a secondary tense in the indicative mood.

- Third class condition: the condition *as uncertain of fulfillment*, but still likely. The third-class condition encompasses a broad semantic range: a logical connection (if A, then B) in the present time (sometimes called present general condition), indicating nothing as to the fulfillment of the protasis; a mere hypothetical situation or one that probably will not be fulfilled; a more probable future occurrence.

- Fourth class condition (less probable future): a possible condition in the future, usually a remote possibility (such as if he could do something, if perhaps this should occur). The protasis involves εἰ + the optative mood. The optative is also used in the apodosis along with ἄν (to indicate contingency).

- What is the best translation for the word ἐκλέγομαι?
    - I choose, select

- What is the best translation for the word σπέρμα?
    - Seed, offspring

- What is the best translation for the word σκάνδαλον?
    - Trap, temptation to sin

- What is the best translation for the word πλήν?
    - But, yet, however

- What is the best translation for the word ἐπιτιμάω?
    - I rebuke, warn

- What is the best translation for the word προστίθημι?
    - I add to, increase, grant

- What is the best translation for the word ἐλευθερόω?
    - I am free, set free

- What is the best translation for the word πορνεία?
  - Prostitution, fornication
- What is the best translation for the word σήμερον?
  - Today
- What is the best translation for the word αὔριον?
  - Tomorrow, the next day

Quiz

1. The "if" part of a conditional sentence is called the . . .
    a) Apodosis
    b) Protasis
    c) Apposition
    d) Consequence

2. The "then" part of a conditional sentence is called the . . .
    a) Protasis
    b) Apposition
    c) Apodosis
    d) Consequence

3. A first-class condition is:
    a) Contrary to fact
    b) Assumed true for argument's sake
    c) Uncertain, but still likely
    d) Less probable future

4. A second-class condition is:
    a) Contrary to fact
    b) Assumed true for argument's sake
    c) Uncertain, but still likely
    d) Less probable future

5. A third-class condition is:

a) Contrary to fact
b) Assumed true for argument's sake
c) Uncertain, but still likely
d) Less probable future

6. The following sentence is an example of which class condition: ἐάν τις περιπατῇ ἐν τῇ ἡμέρᾳ, οὐ προσκόπτει (stumble)?

    a) First class
    b) Second class
    c) Third class
    d) Fourth class

7. The following sentence is an example of which class condition: εἰ καὶ πάντες σκανδαλισθήσονται (they fall away), ἀλλ' οὐκ ἐγώ?

    a) First class
    b) Second class
    c) Third class
    d) Fourth class

8. The following sentence is an example of which class condition: καὶ εἰ μὴ ἐκολόβωσεν (he cut short) κύριος τὰς ἡμέρας, οὐκ ἂν ἐσώθη πᾶσα σάρξ?

    a) First class
    b) Second class
    c) Third class
    d) Fourth class

9. The following sentence is an example of which class condition: τί ἂν θέλοι ὁ σπερμολόγος (babbler) οὗτος λέγειν?

    a) First class
    b) Second class
    c) Third class
    d) Fourth class

10. Why did Paul use a first-class conditional sentence in this example: εἰ δὲ ἀνάστασις νεκρῶν οὐκ ἔστιν, οὐδὲ Χριστὸς ἐγήγερται?

    a) Because this is a contrary-to-fact condition
    b) Because the statement is assumed true for argument's sake

c) Because Paul wants to stress the certainness of the statement ("since ...")
d) Because Paul is stressing the condition as a "future less certain"

ANSWER KEY

1. B, 2. C, 3. B, 4. A, 5. C, 6. C, 7. A, 8. B, 9. D, 10. B

Notes